NATIONAL GEOGRAPHIC

Bricks, Wood and Stones

Mario Lucca

This is my house.

It's made from bricks.

Bricks come from clay.

Clay comes from the ground.

This is my house.

It's made from wood.

Wood comes from trees.

Trees grow in the ground.

This is my house.

It's made from stones.

Stones come from the ground.

Bricks, wood and stones make strong houses.